The Ballad of Scarborough Shoal

Sen. Francis Tol Tolentino

A Tolentino Maritime Publications Book

The Ballad of Scarborough Shoal

Bajo de Masinloc Poems

This is not simply a poetry collection. It is:

- *A poetic narrative of Scarborough Shoal / Bajo de Masinloc*
- *A historical defense grounded in maps and law*
- *A tribute to Filipino fisherfolk and men in uniform*
- *A reflection on sovereignty and maritime law*
- *A spiritual stewardship piece about the sea*
- *A nationalistic yet internationally framed work*

Printed in the United States of America

First Edition, 2026

Dedication

To the Filipino people - and to all nations born of the sea, bound by its tides, sustained by its depths, and protected by the laws written in its name.

Table of Contents

The Shoal Exists

15°9.120′N, 117°46.228′E

Before argument,
before patrol boats,
before declarations and dashed lines,

there was a triangle of reef
lifting itself
1.8 meters
above high tide.

South Rock —
a shoulder of coral
barely taller
than a man standing upright,
yet older
than any flag
that would one day try
to claim it.

Forty-six kilometers
of broken rim.

One hundred fifty square kilometers
of quiet lagoon.

A ring of teeth
encircling blue.

Two islets.
Many reefs.
No population.
No city.
No monument.

Only salt.
Only wind.
Only tide repeating its argument
with stone.

Two hundred twenty kilometers
from Luzon —
close enough
that fishermen measure the distance
in fuel,
in weather,
in memory.

Between the shoal and shore
the Manila Trench
falls

five thousand meters
into darkness —

as if the earth itself
opened its mouth
and kept its silence.

Long before anyone
would call it

Panacot,
Bajo de Masinloc,
Panatag,
Scarborough —

it was only coral
and current,
a geometry of patience
rising
where the sea decided
to pause.

It does not shout.

It does not rise like a mountain.

It waits.

1.8 meters above surrender.

The Velarde Map (1734)

Before patrol boats,
before tribunals,
before dashed lines drawn in red,

there was ink.

1734.

A Jesuit hand
measuring coastlines
with patience and brass instruments,
charting islands
that had already learned
the grammar of tide.

Off the coast of Central Luzon
one primary name clearly appeared:

Panacot.

Not shouted.
Not argued.
Simply written.

Panacot —
a shoal in quiet proximity
to a shore already known.

The parchment did not tremble.
It did not foresee
water cannons
or microphones.

It recorded.

Longitude sketched in certainty.
Latitude resting beside it
like a fact too ordinary
to contest.

In Madrid,
in Manila,
in archives where dust moves slower than politics,
the reef endured in ink.

Maps do not declare war.
They declare position.

A line drawn in 1734
is not prophecy.

It is memory

pressed into paper.

And paper,
when folded carefully
and passed through centuries,

outlives
noise.

My Maps

Author is shown with his two Original Maps

I did not find them
in an archive.

One I found

on a sidewalk
in the Netherlands —
rolled tight,
creased with travel.

The other
in a small shop in Paris,
hung between engravings
of rivers and forgotten ports.

One dated 1820.
The other 1835.

Different cities.
Different hands.

The same reef
resting west of Luzon.

Ink browned
to the color of old tea.

When I unrolled them
on a table
far from Luzon,
the reef was there —

small,
deliberate,

placed without drama
west of Zambales.

Not highlighted.
Not circled.
Simply present.

Bajo de Masinloc.

The name resting
as if it had never expected
to be questioned.

My fingers followed
the faint coastline
of Central Luzon,
moved westward
across blank sea,

and stopped
on a scatter of coral
drawn by someone
who had never imagined
a standoff,
a press conference,
a broadcast at sea.

Maps are not loud.

They whisper in contour lines.

They crease where they are folded.
They soften where hands have held them.

These maps have traveled
longer than I have.

They have survived
more empires
than I have known.

And yet here they are —
paper thin,
fragile at the edges,

carrying a reef
that rises
1.8 meters
above tide
and far higher
in memory.

I do not raise my voice
over them.

I smooth the fold.

I let the ink

speak
at its own pace.

The Old Waves

Before maps were folded
and stored in drawers,

before ink decided
where land ended
and water began,

the waves already knew.

They broke against coral
in patterns older than empire.

They curved along the rim
of a lagoon
that had never heard
the word sovereignty.

The sea does not recognize
dash lines.

It recognizes wind.

It recognizes depth.

It remembers the trench
falling five thousand meters
into shadow
between Luzon
and the shoal.

Currents moved west
long before arguments
moved east.

Storms passed over
without choosing sides.

Salt gathered in the same places
year after year
until fishermen learned
how to read it
like scripture.

The waves that touch Panatag
have touched
a thousand hulls —

Spanish frigates,
merchant vessels,
wooden bancas,
steel patrol boats.

The water did not change its tone.

It rose.
It fell.

It returned.

Even now
when microphones lean toward it
and cameras watch the horizon,

the old waves continue
their patient grammar

breaking,
retreating,
breaking again.

Traditional Fishing Ground

Before coordinates
were printed in books,
before cases were filed
in distant courts,

boats left the shore at dawn.

Wood against tide.
Oar against current.
Men reading wind
the way others read law.

They did not call it
exclusive economic zone.

They called it
where the fish are.

Two hundred twenty kilometers
is not a theory
when fuel is counted
in borrowed pesos.

The reef was known
by weather.

By the way the water changed color
just before the lagoon.

By the shift in current
that told them
where coral rose
just beneath the hull.

Grandfathers spoke of it
without raising their voices.

Not as conquest.
Not as entitlement.

But as inheritance.

A place where nets returned heavy.
Where storms could be outrun
if the wind held steady.

Panatag.

Serene sandbank.

The name carried
not the weight of dispute,
but the rhythm of return.

When tribunals later wrote
of traditional fishing rights,
they used careful language.

But the fishermen
had already known.

They measured ownership
in seasons.

In calloused hands.

In mornings that began
long before politics
woke up.

The Ramming

It did not begin
with a headline.

It began with wood.

A small bangka
rocking gently
in water that had always
been read as livelihood.

Nets drawn in.
Engines low.
The long wait between haul and horizon.

Then steel entered the frame.

Not conversation.
Not warning.

Just weight.

A hull too large
to pretend

it had not seen
what lay before it.

The sound was not dramatic.

No orchestra.
No declaration.

Only the blunt language
of impact —

wood split,
outriggers twisted,
water rising faster
than hands could measure.

A man does not argue
with a wave.

He does not argue
with steel either.

He grabs for rope.
For another shoulder.
For air.

The lagoon that once held
their fathers' nets
held something else that day —

shock,
diesel,
the quick silence
that follows collision.

Boats can be repaired.

Wood can be replaced.

But a name called out
across water
does not always return.

There are distances
no engine can cross.

And when the sea settles
after violence,

it settles
without apology.

The Wake

Author attending The Wake of a Fisherman who died because his boat was rammed

I did not meet him
at sea.

I met him
in a room
lit by candles
and electric fans
that turned slowly
above grief.

There is a different tide
in a wake.

It rises
in the eyes of a mother.
It recedes
in the silence of a daughter
who has not yet learned
how to hold absence.

The sea had already taken
what it would take.

What remained
was wood framed in white,
photographs placed
carefully beside flowers,
a name spoken
more softly
than before.

I listened
to stories of nets,
of weather read by instinct,
of mornings that began
while the rest of the town
still slept.

No one mentioned
international law.

No one spoke
of nautical miles.

They spoke of school fees.
Of fuel.
Of the way he laughed
when the catch was good.

There are arguments
best left outside
a house of mourning.

Inside,
there is only the arithmetic
of loss.

I placed a laptop
in the hands
of his eldest daughter.

It was not a solution.

It was a bridge —
thin,
necessary,
human.

In that room
I understood something
no tribunal writes clearly:

A reef is not only coral.

It is consequence.

And when a boat
does not return whole,

the damage travels
farther
than water.

The Bangkas

Author Donating Bangkas to Fishermen of Masinloc, Zambales, 2024

Wood is lighter than steel.

It carries more than weight —
it carries return.

After the wake,
after the quiet arithmetic
of loss,

there were hulls to shape.

In Masinloc
they build them narrow and balanced,
outriggers stretching outward
like steady hands.

Bangkas.

Not monuments.
Not statements.

Tools.

A plank fitted to a frame.
A keel laid straight.
An engine tested
against tide.

I stood beside men
who measure hope
in plywood and paint,
in bolts tightened
with salt on their wrists.

A boat does not erase
what happened.

It does not rewrite
the sound of impact.

But it answers it.

It says:
we will go out again.

We will not surrender
a horizon
that has fed us
for generations.

When the first bangka
slid back into water,
there was no speech.

Only a push
from shore,

and that quiet moment
when wood meets sea
and does not sink.

Some acts are small
enough to miss
on satellite images.

They do not appear
in official statements.

But a rebuilt boat

entering a familiar current
is its own declaration —

not shouted,
not waved,

simply carried forward
on tide.

Masinloc

The town does not face headlines.

It faces west.

Houses low against wind,
boats pulled high against storm,
children running barefoot
between nets hung out to dry.

Masinloc is not a courtroom.

It is mornings before sun,
coffee strong and bitter,
engines coughing awake
while the sky is still undecided.

Here, the shoal is not
an argument.

It is direction.

West until the water changes color.
West until the lagoon appears

like a breath held
inside the sea.

The fishermen speak of it
as if speaking of weather —

ordinary,
necessary,
known.

In small stores along the road,
conversations bend
toward tides and fuel prices,
toward cousins who have not returned
as early as they should have.

The shoal lives here
in quiet calculations:

How far?
How long?
How much diesel?
How much risk?

The town remembers
every season of calm
and every season of steel.

It remembers when access

was simple,
when the lagoon opened
without negotiation.

It remembers
when it did not.

Masinloc carries the reef
in its posture —
shoulders squared against wind,
eyes always measuring
the horizon.

Maps may label the shoal
with foreign names.

But here,
it is only the place
their fathers taught them
to find by instinct.

And when dusk falls
over the western edge of town,

the boats return
one by one,

bringing with them
not just fish,

but proof
that memory
still sails.

The Standoff

It began
with boats facing boats.

Not guns raised.
Not sirens.

Just hull against horizon,
distance measured
in meters
and restraint.

The lagoon entrance
is narrow —
a mouth
through which water breathes.

That day
it became a threshold.

A vessel anchored.
Another arrived.
Radios carried words

carefully chosen
and carefully doubted.

Agreement was spoken.

Both parties would leave.

The tide shifted.

One side did not.

After that,
presence became routine.

White hulls at the rim.
Uniforms visible
through binoculars.

Fishermen approaching slowly,
waiting to see
if the lagoon would open
or remain watched.

There are confrontations
that explode.

This one endured.

No declaration of war.
No formal surrender.

Only days becoming months,
months becoming years,

until the extraordinary
learned to call itself
normal.

The shoal did not move.

It remained
1.8 meters above high tide,
as it had in 1734,
as it had in 1820,
as it had in every map
that marked it quietly.

But something invisible
had shifted —

access.

Not ownership declared,
but access controlled.

The difference
is subtle in language.

It is not subtle
on water.

Boats still left Masinloc.

They simply left
with uncertainty.

And uncertainty,
when it repeats itself long enough, hardens
into fact.

Maritime Zones Law

An island state is drawn by sea,
its breath in salted air;
its borders are not fenced by land,
but measured deep and fair.

From baselines traced along the coast
where tides advance and fall,
the law extends in ordered reach
beyond the harbor wall.

Not conquest, nor expanding will,
nor sudden claim of might;
but codified in careful text,
in articles precise and tight.

An archipelago must move
through channels shaped by rule;
sea lanes acknowledged in respect,
not governed by a duel.

Domestic statute joins the tide
to conventions overseas;

what is written into law at home
speaks also on the seas.

A shoal may rise a meter high,
a reef may barely show,
yet jurisdiction does not rest
on height alone, but so:

On governance declared and kept,
on duties understood,
on stewardship of maritime trust
for common, lasting good.

The sea is wide; the code is clear;
the measure is not flame —
it is the steady architecture
that gives a coast its name.

The Exclusive Economic Zone

Two hundred nautical miles from measured shore
where baseline meets the sea,
the law confers a living trust —
not reach of tyranny.

It grants the right to harvest well
what nature there has grown,
to guard the reefs and spawning grounds
as if they were one's own.

Not every swell is territory,
not every crest a claim;
but stewardship within those bounds
is duty, not a game.

Beneath the shoal the coral builds
cathedrals slow and bright;
each fragile branch in patient tiers
constructs its silent height.

A reef once broken does not heal

in seasons short or mild;
it mends in decades, sometimes more,
like memory defiled.

The zone is more than numbered miles,
more than a charted ring;
it is the pledge to future hands
of what the seas may bring.

Fish that school in silver arcs,
larvae drifting free,
currents carrying unseen life
through hidden nursery.

So when the water clouds with sand
and coral turns to scar,
the injury extends beyond
whatever borders are.

Two hundred nautical miles is not excess,
nor boundary drawn in greed;
it is the space where care must stand
against destructive speed.

For law that measures depth and span
must answer what is lost —
not only who may cast a net,
but who will bear the cost.

Water Cannons

No gunfire split the morning air,
no smoke obscured the sky;
just arcs of pressurized white force
against a hull riding high.

A blast of water, cold and hard,
meant not to kill, but warn;
yet force by any other name
is still a thing outworn.

The spray rose up like broken glass,
then crashed against the deck;
a smaller boat rocked in its wake,
its balance held in check.

No bullet pierced the timber frame,
no flame consumed the mast;
but pressure carries its own weight
when steel meets wood at last.

The world may say it is restraint
because no life was claimed;

yet violence need not draw blood
for power to be named.

A floating line across the sea,
a barrier drawn by spray —
control asserted not by ink
but by the force of day.

Still, vessels turned and faced the surge,
not reckless, not undone;
for dignity does not retreat
because of water's run.

The shoal remained, 1.8 high,
untouched by blast or roar;
and tides resumed their ancient work
as they had done before.

Chant of the Sea

Bless the Scarborough Shoal.
Bless the sea that breathes around the shoal.

Bless the current that remembers
what ink forgets.

Bless the coral rising
grain by grain,
year by patient year.

Bless the reef
before it was argued.

Bless the reef
after it was named.

Let the tide return.
Let the tide return.

Not in anger.
In order.

Bless the fishermen who read the wind

without compass,
without decree.

Bless the hands that mend the nets.

Bless the hands that hold the rope
when water turns against them.

Let the lagoon remain open.
Let the lagoon remain living.

Not emptied by haste.
Not scarred by greed.

Bless the trench that falls unseen
between shore and shoal,
five thousand meters of silence
holding the weight of history.

Bless the guardians who patrol at dawn,
who stand without spectacle,
who watch without shouting.

Let restraint be stronger than steel.
Let patience outlast pressure.

Bless the sea.
Bless the sea that outlives empires.

For it was here

before maps were drawn,

and it will remain
after arguments tire.

Bless the shoal,
1.8 meters above tide,
rising not in fury,
but in persistence.

Bless what feeds.
Bless what shelters.
Bless what endures.

Let the sea be sea.

Let the sea be sea.

The Reefs

They do not rise in haste.

They build in whispers,
in latticed light,
in patient mineral memory.

Branch by branch,
bone by bone,
a city of color
beneath a skin of blue.

Polyp and pulse,
calcium and current,
a cathedral grown
from the smallest insistence.

What seems like stone
is living.

What looks like silence
is speech in slow syllables —
reef repeating reef,

layer answering layer.

Parrotfish graze in green arcs.
Silver schools shimmer and scatter.
Larvae drift like prayers
carried farther than nets.

The reef remembers
warm seasons and cooler ones,
storm surge and still water,
the shadow of hulls passing overhead.

It does not choose flags.

It chooses balance.

Too much heat,
it pales.

Too much dredging,
it breaks.

Too much hurry,
it scars.

Yet left in rhythm —
tide, sun, dark, tide —
it returns to brightness,
returns to branching light.

A reef is architecture
without blueprint,
order without proclamation.

It feeds what feeds us.

It shelters what shelters us.

And when its color fades,
something in the sea
falls quiet.

Not dramatic.
Not loud.

Just diminished.

So let it grow in measured peace.
Let it knit itself back to wholeness.
Let its hidden cities stand

longer
than dispute.

The Philippine Coast Guard in Panatag

They rise before the light does.

Engines turn over
while the horizon is still gray.

No anthem plays.
No crowd gathers.

Just coordinates entered.
Fuel checked.
Radios tested.

They move west.

White hull cutting
through familiar water,
through uncertainty
that has learned to repeat itself.

Their work is not spectacle.

It is distance maintained.
Distance recorded.

Distance endured.

They do not shout sovereignty.

They log it.

Time.
Latitude.
Encounter.

They stand on decks
that rock but do not yield,
eyes steady on vessels
larger, louder,
painted with authority.

Orders are simple:
hold position.
observe.
return safely.

Not charge.
Not provoke.

Hold.

There is courage
in not escalating.

There is discipline

in restraint.

They patrol the edge
of a reef that rises
barely above tide
yet higher
than fear.

When spray hits the bow,
they do not answer with fury.

They answer
with presence.

White against blue.
Steady against surge.

They rise before the light does.

And when they return
to harbor,

the sea closes behind them
without applause.

Ode to the Philippine Navy

They sail where deeper waters roll,
where currents press and strain;
steel hulls cut through heavier seas
with patience, not with pain.

Their decks are broad, their shadows long
across the shifting foam;
yet power need not bare its teeth
to signal it has come.

They watch where smaller vessels stand
near coral barely high;
a reef that lifts a meter's height
beneath an open sky.

Across the rim of Panatag
larger silhouettes may loom;
gray against a brighter sea,
imposing in their plume.

But discipline is not a shout,
nor strength a reckless thrust;

it is the tempered steadiness
of duty joined to trust.

They hold the line of presence firm
where law and water meet;
not seeking flame nor spectacle,
but stance that will not retreat.

The sea remembers every wake
that passed across its span;
it measures not the tonnage first,
but purpose behind man.

And so they move in ordered calm
through channels tight and wide;
for sovereignty need not be loud
to anchor in the tide.

Archipelagic Sea Lanes

An island chain is not confined
to shore where breakers fall;
its breath extends through winding straits
that link the whole to all.

From north to south, from east to west,
through channels deep and wide,
the archipelago must move
in lawful, open stride.

Sea lanes drawn in mutual trust,
acknowledged, clear, defined —
not barriers set in sudden haste,
nor corridors confined.

For islands scattered over blue
must live by ordered way;
the waters joining land to land
cannot be locked away.

Respect the course that vessels take
through passages agreed;

let transit flow in peaceful form
without coercive speed.

An archipelago is whole
when sea and shore align;
its unity not just in sand,
but in the channels' spine.

So let the lanes remain secure,
their compass steady still;
for sovereignty is strongest where
it governs without will

to choke the passage others use
in lawful, balanced frame —
a nation firm within its bounds
need not inflame its claim.

The sea that binds the islands close
must also open be;
for freedom in the wider world
begins in ordered sea.

Scarborough as Event

There are events that flare and fade,
that burn and then are gone;
and there are events that settle in
and quietly move on.

Not into past, but into pulse,
into the daily chart —
an argument that does not sleep
but lives inside the heart.

Scarborough is not a date
circled on a page;
it is a chapter still being writ
in law, in tide, in age.

It lives in hulls that face each other
at the lagoon's small gate;
it lives in maps re-read at night,
in notes that annotate.

It lives in fishermen who weigh
the cost of going west;

in coast guards marking coordinates
with vigilance as test.

An event can be a single spark,
a clash, a shouted claim;
or it can be a long endurance
that refuses to inflame.

This reef has entered history
not as a passing scene,
but as a measure of how states
will hold what they have been.

For history is not always war,
nor treaty signed and sealed;
sometimes it is a steady stand
where neither side will yield.

Scarborough rises from the tide
no higher than before;
yet it has grown in consequence
far greater than its shore.

An event is what we call the hour
when choices crystallize —
when patience proves its lasting strength
before impatient eyes.

And so the reef becomes a test
of posture more than might:
of who can stand in measured calm
and who must escalate.

It will not vanish from the page
nor sink beneath debate;
for some events are not concluded —
they simply navigate.

What Scarborough Should Be

Let the shoal remain
open to lawful passage.

Let the lagoon breathe
without barrier or fear.

Let fishermen enter at dawn
and leave at dusk
with nets earned by labor,
not granted by permission.

Let the reef grow
in color, not in scar.

Let coral branch in quiet light
untroubled by haste.

Let the sea lanes remain clear,
their courses honored,
their transit peaceful.

Let no nation mistake
restraint for weakness.

Let no vessel confuse
size with right.

Let law stand taller
than spray.

Let maps be read
in their time
and respected in ours.

Let memory outlast
pressure.

Let sovereignty mean
care before claim,
duty before display.

Let Masinloc face west
without anxiety.

Let Bangkas return
with steady engines
and unbroken hulls.

Let the Coast Guard sail
without provocation.

Let the Navy hold
without escalation.

Let the trench remain
a depth of silence,
not of threat.

Let the shoal rise
1.8 meters above tide
and far above surrender.

Let Scarborough be
not a flashpoint,
but a promise —

that an island people
can stand firm
without shouting,

can defend
without hatred,

can endure
without losing grace.

Let the sea be sea.

Let it be living.

Let it be shared
in law,
in order,

in peace.

Epistle to the Filipino People

Mga Minamahal Kong Kababayan,

I do not write to you
from a podium.

I write from a shoreline
that faces west.

You have read the headlines.
You have seen the footage —
boats, barriers,
water rising against hulls.

But I want you to remember
what came before the noise.

The maps in quiet ink.
The fishermen at dawn.
The reef rising patient
above tide.

This shoal is not
an abstract dispute.

It is a place your fathers sailed to
without asking permission.

It is a horizon measured
in diesel and faith.

Some will say
it is too small to matter.

1.8 meters above water.

Barely visible on a clear day.

But we are an island people.

We know that what rises only slightly
can still anchor a nation.

I have stood in Masinloc
and listened to widows speak softly.

I have watched young men
push Bangkas back into sea
because retreat is not inheritance.

This is not a call to anger.

Anger is brief.

This is a call to memory.

Memory lasts longer than spray.

We must remain steady.
Steadier than steel.

We must remain lawful.
Stronger than provocation.

We must remain patient.
Longer than pressure.

For sovereignty is not
how loudly we answer, but how consistently
we return.

Mahal kong Kababayan, the sea that sur-
rounds us
is not merely border.

It is breath.

Guard it without hatred.
Defend it without fury.
Hold it without fear.

And when you look west- across the West
Philippine Sea at dusk,

Remember Scarborough Shoal-

not large upon the earth,

yet enduring upon the soul of a Nation.

With you always,

Tol

Francis Tol Tolentino

www.ingramcontent.com/pod-product-compliance
Lightning Source LLC
LaVergne TN
LVHW090617110826
845146LV00001B/425

* 9 7 9 8 9 9 3 8 6 4 6 5 5 *